A Guide for Volunteers Teaching English as a Second Language

Language as a vehicle to integration

Local Immigration Partnership
Partenariat local pour l'immigration
LANARK & RENFREW

Content Contributors:
Lana Johnston
Marja Huis
Chela Breckon
Cameron Montgomery
Sabrina Farmer
Conor Leggett
Laura Julien

Editorial Team:
Chela Breckon
Marja Huis
Lana Johnston

2nd Edition Layout and Design by Studio Dreamshare Press (publishing@studiodreamshare.com) based on branding identity guidelines by Design House (betty@design-house.ca).

ISBN: 978-1-7753943-5-8
2nd Edition. Copyleft. Open source.
Local Immigration Partnership Lanark & Renfrew
Community Settlement Initiative
Canadian Red Cross
Algonquin College – Pembroke Campus
For content inquiries, please contact https://liplanarkrenfrew.ca.

For editorial publishing notations please contact publishing@studiodreamshare.com.

STUDIO DREAMSHARE PRESS
18 Pembroke St. W, Pembroke, Ontario
www.StudioDreamsharePress.com

Table of Contents

Introduction 4
Motivation 6
Adversity 14
Priority & Preference 22
Strategy 30
Learning Tactic Cards 40

THE COMMUNITY LANGUAGE SUPPORT MODEL

Algonquin College and ESL experts, with funding from The Canadian Red Cross, have created a new language-learning delivery model called the Community Language Support Program.

The program is a decentralized, place-based approach to language learning where community members teach English in ways that directly support the individual learner. It is done in the places and spaces they choose to live in and according to their schedule and preference for learning.

The program is a response to traditional challenges inherent in offering English-as-a-Second-Language training to adult newcomers, especially in rural areas. Roadblocks along their language learning journey include transportation, childcare, hours of service, eligibility requirements, funding requirements such as minimum numbers of regularly attending registrants, and so on. These challenges cannot be alleviated by a centralized or singular nature of service delivery—one place, one way and at one time.

Instead, the program effectively and efficiently leaps over these common barriers. No new infrastructure is required and the work is delivered by community allies. These volunteers are supported by a qualified Language Coach who provides access to key supports, resources, suggested tactics and materials to build their capacity to teach.

By combining the good nature of volunteer work to the meaningful purpose for adult newcomers to learn English that is supported by a professional creates a holistic and sustainable community-wide program.

The newcomers are integrated as defined by themselves. The volunteer is empowered to support both as a humanitarian and as a capable ally. Community relationships enhance connections among the people involved, transforming language learning into a vehicle for integration.

How You Use This Handbook

Supporting an adult learning a new language is a dynamic journey that can only be approached with the learner in mind at all times. Traditional classroom-style learning may not be the most effective way to teach or absorb information for everyone. In fact, allies within the community such as volunteers, friends and support agents (like you!) who directly focus on the reasons why a learner wants to learn English and address their unique challenges along the way, is the most promising practice. Language-learning allies can help select learning priorities and tactics to create meaningful, intentional and personalized learning strategies. As community allies, we invite you to use this handbook as a roadmap for the language learning journey. You can follow the M.A.P.S. framework to plan your course of action for the most effective results.

Motivation: Why learn English

Adversity: What challenges

Priority & Preference: What to focus on, and when and where to learn

Strategy: How to learn

Each chapter has a PB&J moment.

The old-fashioned peanut butter and jelly sandwich have been a staple when we are busy and need a quick solution. Our language learning PB&J moments are meant to check our **Privilege, Bias & Judgement**. They are meant for us to step back and assess the thoughts and ideas that inform our actions and decisions. It will help you as an ally to see yourself in the language learning journey: Am I able to see the learner's actual barriers? Does my life experience or situation privilege, limit or enhance my empathy for the learner's journey/life?

Why Learn English?

Let's find out what motivates the learner! It's more than goal setting: We must find out why a learner has a specific destination in mind.

Sounds difficult? It is actually the easiest and first step to language learning in the M.A.P.S. framework: Ask the learner why they are on this language learning journey and together you will discover their desired destination.

Identifying motivation is about more than setting goals. You need to investigate why a learner wants to improve their English.

Here are examples of what you can ask to determine your learner's language goals, along with sample answers that have been collected from adult language learners:

1. Why do you want to learn English?
To chat with people and make friends. **(GOAL)**

2. Why does that matter to you?
Because I want to join some clubs and social groups to have fun. **(GOAL)**

3. Why does social life and fun matter to you?
Because I want to feel like I belong – I want to feel at home here. **(PURPOSE)**

The Bigger Picture

You can see that the first two responses above are more like goals, but when you probe deeper you discover that these are driven by the human need to belong and feel comfortable in the new place they call home. When people can find the highest purpose behind their chosen goals, it is easier to motivate because the desire comes from within and is connected to something much bigger than learning English.
Referring back to this ultimate purpose driving the effort is essential to success. Learning goals are fluid in any person's life as they develop or the need arises to reshape them, yet the purpose driving the dynamic goal remains unchanged.

"My Happy Place", Brooklyn Sullivan, *Shukraan Community Arts Workshop*, Studio Dreamshare, 2019.

TIP

Determine the learner's emotional reasons (Purpose) for learning English, because these feed and sustain their motivation. Examples:
   "I want to read English books with my daughter so we can enjoy our time together."
   "I want to learn English well enough to play sports and go out for drinks with friends."
   "I want to get a job as a healthcare practitioner and need to be competent in English."

GOAL	PURPOSE
- It's part of the agreement with my sponsorship group that brought me to Canada. - To improve my quality of life. - To find employment. - To get a better job. - To read English newspapers. - To surf the internet for fun (read online articles/ watch YouTube videos/follow my favs on social media. - To go to school (go to university or college). - To travel to other countries and within Canada. - To understand my favourite songs and watch movies in English. - I was offered free English lessons! - I enjoy learning English and other languages. - My significant other speaks English. - To be closer to Canadian culture.	- I want to respect the sponsors by demonstrating gratitude through effort. - I want my kids to have a better life. - I want to be able to support my family. - I want to feel self-worth. - I want to feel normal and fit in with my colleagues. - I want to belong to a group of friends. - I want to be able to live to my full potential here in Canada. - I want to live my fullest life. - I don't want to feel so different all the time. - I can get what I need independently without burdening my family or friends. - I want to feel normal like back home, doing things I love. - I want to deepen my relationship with my spouse and children who speak English. - I want to feel truly at home in Canada one day.

WHY IS IT IMPORTANT FOR LEARNERS TO SET PERSONAL LANGUAGE GOALS?

Learner motivation is paramount in language learning for everyone involved, including supports such as teachers and family members.

Identifying personal language goals provides a road map and a destination for the language learning journey.

When a learner is determined to achieve their own goals, they can focus and are productive for longer periods of time.

When the learner sees progress towards one of their personal goals, it builds confidence and encourages them to continue achieving milestones.

Because of this, learners tend to enjoy their language learning journey more, which contributes to their success.

"Home", Joanne Allgoewer, *Shukraan Community Arts Workshop*, Studio Dreamshare, 2019.

TIP

Learning English is enormously beneficial to your learner. The ability to communicate will be key to their well-being, including community integration, employment, education and making Canada their new home.

HOW CAN YOU KEEP LEARNERS FOCUSED ON THEIR PERSONAL LANGUAGE GOALS?

Return to the purpose of learning English whenever possible. Use images or symbols of the true reason why they are learning English to help connect the tough days to the bigger picture.

Ask your learner to post their language goals where others can see them too. Family members and house guests, for example, can be a huge source of support in staying motivated.

Remind your learner to reward themselves for each milestone reached, big and small. Also, track progress to instill pride in how far they have come on their language learning journey.

Stay curious yourself: ask your learner open questions and listen actively, inquire about inconsistencies you may have noticed, or recognize changes you see along the way. Encourage them to do the same!

Help your learner create a routine that involves making time to practice every day and incorporate English into their daily routine.

Explore different teaching methods and do not be afraid to make mistakes, but apply what you've learned.

Be patient: Learning a language is a long and tough road! Figure out a "brain break" when needed and help your learner refocus when the going gets tough. Encourage getting active, connecting with a loved one, exploring self-care and taking steps to create that same peaceful space in English.

Have fun! Your learner will better succeed when they enjoy the process and see the tangible results.

PB&J MOMENT
(Privilege, Bias & Judgement)

Put Your Own Agenda Aside

A desire to learn is fueled by personal motivation. To effectively support a learner, you need to put your own agenda aside and discover the personal motivation of the learner.

By asking open-ended questions you and the learner will identify not only the overall motivation to learn but also specific learning goals. You need to adopt these goals as your own to enable the language learner to succeed.

For example, you may imagine the most important learning goal is passing a driver's test, but your learner may strongly desire the ability to communicate with their child's teacher. If you and the learner work at cross purposes, the learning journey will likely not be successful.

By bringing the learner's personal motivation to light, their learning journey will have a much better chance of success.

STORYTIME!

A group of volunteers have shared a story about a learner who was mandated to go to an English class by his sponsorship group's contract for the first year.

Unfortunately, the young man did not seem motivated to learn English. He was always tired, showed up late for class, refused to read or write and was apathetic towards any lesson even when it involved "fun" activities and games.

Then, on the way to an appointment in Ottawa, a volunteer driver had a simple conversation with the young father about what he wanted to do. In broken English and using hand gestures, he explained that he wanted a job to drive a car and support his family.

On their next adventure a few weeks later, the volunteer mentioned a small weekend job opportunity. Even though he would earn little money, the young man's posture and attitude changed completely. He had a light in his eyes.

Since he did not have a car or a license, the volunteer drove the young man to and from his odd jobs around the area on weekends. While driving, the volunteer would point out road signs, indicators or lights on the dashboard and ask the young man to repeat the words in English.

A few months later, the volunteer without any teaching experience had successfully taught the young man English driving vocabulary and conversational skills simply by paying attention to the learner's personal purpose which would drive his motivation. The young father got his driver's license and has become an outgoing member of the community. Not surprisingly, the volunteer has become a close friend of the family!

What's the difference between external and internal motivation?

External "The Carrot" – an incentive that is attractive to a person that they will earn if they complete the task.

PRO: Rewards are fun ways to signal and symbolize accomplishments.

CON: The attractiveness and value of the incentive are situational and can quickly change.

Internal "The Drive" – something within a person that pushes them to keep going and finish the task, usually something bigger than the task itself like passion, purpose and values.

PRO: Connect the daily grind to a much bigger purpose or reason to do something, normally the most powerful way to motivate.

CON: Can be hard to figure out for yourself and others without intentionality.

"A New Horizon", Jana Jaros, *Shukraan Community Arts Workshop*, Studio Dreamshare, 2019.

What challenges?

No matter how motivated we are – learner and volunteer– there are bound to be times when we feel discouraged or are grappling with life's challenges.

Sound familiar? These are the times we need to take a step back to assess, analyze and adapt. Ask the learner about obstacles and help them find solutions. Ask yourself about your challenges and capacity to teach and support in addition to what self-care you might need.

Barriers Beyond Language

Language skills like reading and writing help learners navigate the world around them, from shopping and paying bills to making friends and participating in the community. Aside from challenges related to language, learners simultaneously have to manage many other hurdles that can impede their progress on the language learning journey.
When reviewing the following paragraphs, consider how each of the situations might be a challenge and/or an opportunity for language training.

Employment & Volunteering

Canadian society and the Canadian economy may be new to a large percentage of learners, including how to apply for jobs and build experience. Volunteering may be a new concept altogether. Yet these are all important steps for newcomers to gain financial independence and access to social networks. A learner who works 40 hours per week may have little time to learn English. However, there could be an opportunity to incorporate language learning as a component of the job with the help of a supportive employer.

Childcare & Schooling

Learners with families support their children in adapting to a new place. Often children outpace their parents in learning a new language thanks to immersion in school with other children, and a higher capacity for learning new concepts than adults. This may provide a good opportunity for adult learners to learn alongside their children. Other considerations may include the parents' preference to retain their native language in the home, and difficulty accessing childcare.

Physical & Mental Health

Studies have identified the "Healthy Immigrant Effect," whereby newcomers tend to be healthier than the domestic population upon arriving in Canada, but their health tends to deteriorate to a level below their Canadian-born counterparts (Edward Ng, 2015, https://www.150statcan.gc.ca/n1/pub/82-0-3-x/20110004/article/11588-eng.htm).
Physical and mental health are important factors influencing a learner's ability to commit to learning a second language. It is beneficial for newcomers to be connected with a healthcare provider as soon as possible after arrival to address any major health issues that can impact settlement.

Community Connections & Independence

Learners often want to participate fully in their new home community life. This can be used to motivate learners who may not be interested in sitting in a classroom. The learner who wants to find a job, get a driver's license, or join a sports team often quickly discovers how helpful language skills are in attaining their goal. This provides opportunities for creative ways of learning a language outside the traditional classroom, and in ways that align with a learner's goals.

LIMITING BELIEFS

English is too hard!
I'm not a language learner; I've never done it before.
I'm too busy/tired with parenting, work, etc.
I don't have childcare.
It costs too much.
There are no classes near me.
I don't have a vehicle/license.
My wifi is awful; I don't know how to use a computer or phone.
I just don't know where to start!

Why is it important to ask your learner about their adversities?

- When learners identify why they are not able to succeed, this provides an opportunity for supports to be put in place to eliminate or lessen that particular challenge.

- It gives an opportunity for learners to communicate their struggles, frustrations and fears.

- Sharing potential issues with you in your role as an ally will provide an opportunity for you to build empathy and understanding.

- It validates their feelings.

"Diversity and Inclusion", Tiina Cote, *Shukraan Community Arts Workshop*, Studio Dreamshare, 2019.

What's Normal For You?
Try framing questions in this way when cultural differences come into play.

How do you normally deal with banking and money in your home country?

What is it like to apply for a job where you are from?

What kind of things do children normally do around the home for you?

After learning about the newcomer's experience, the process of sharing how things are usually done in Canada can build understanding while strengthening your relationship with the newcomer.

WHAT ABOUT YOU?
Exploring Your Role as a Volunteer

When exploring your role as a volunteer, it can be helpful to ask yourself some guiding questions: What role will best serve my learner's needs? What role will support the greatest degree of agency and independence for my learners? What role fits within my capacity and limitations?

As a volunteer, you are an integral gift to our society and strengthen many areas of community life.

The benefits of volunteering are enormous to you, your family and the community. The right volunteer role for you will help you make friends, connect with the community, learn new skills, advance a career, and enhance your physical and mental health.

Your role as a volunteer helping families integrate into their new Canadian lifestyle can be both exciting and overwhelming. As a volunteer, you can often find yourself navigating many different roles: teacher, counsellor, friend, parent or tour guide on different days.
Here are some helpful ways to help you navigate your expectations in order to maintain healthy and rewarding relationships with the learners you are supporting.

Connection

Connection is the foundation of any volunteer/learner relationship. At times, you are the first local friend that a newcomer makes when they initially arrive in Canada. The key here is to find a balance between emotional connection and healthy boundary setting. This allows the learner to reach their full potential and helps prevent compassion fatigue and/or burnout.

Your role involves adapting to changing needs, maintaining a strong connection, and embracing "failures" in order to grow and evolve. Your role does not require you to predict and prevent negative outcomes, prevent trial and error and circumvent consequences. Mistakes are going to happen; turn them into opportunities for growth.

Communication

Communicate, communicate, communicate. The key to maintaining connection and understanding each other's expectations in the relationship between yourself and the learner is to communicate, constantly.

Ask your learner and yourself open questions such as:

- ⬢ What is normal for you in this type of situation (housing, financial management, taking care of children, family relationships, etc)?
- ⬢ What is possible for me to do in the short and long term to support your language and settlement goals?
- ⬢ To whom can I outsource tasks outside of my expertise (peer support)?

Be honest that there are no guarantees for success in the relationship between yourself and the learner and avoid over-promising. Saying "no" is also part of this process and requires courage, because it can feel uncomfortable at times.

Communication and honesty will greatly support a relationship between you and the learner that is valuable and dynamic.

Power of Volunteer Peer Connections

Peer support is a powerful tool when volunteers are working with newcomers. Peers offer practical, social and emotional support. Peer connections are the gateway to a community of common interests, shared knowledge, understanding and empathy. An equal (newcomer or volunteer) who shares similar experiences can offer valuable support in a dynamic relationship. Everyone involved benefits from ongoing learning and understanding. Support is mutually offered and reciprocated. These are the rich reviews of peer connections.

STORYTIME!

A newcomer mom with three children was having great difficulty finding time to improve her English. Her husband worked full-time as a manager at a local factory. With two children in school and one toddler, she needed all her time to look after the household.

They could not afford childcare and were not eligible for childcare subsidies.

When the volunteer identified the mother's adversity, she introduced her to the local Early Years Centre that offered a morning drop-in program, as well as afternoon and weekend programs at the local library.

Now the children enjoy being entertained and having fun playing with others, while the volunteer supports the mother in building vocabulary and improving English, all in the same place!

The learner also keeps a photo journal of daily household chores, such as washing the dishes, making coffee, and getting the children to brush their teeth. She brings these to her sessions with the volunteer, which allows them to have specific conversations about the young mother's daily life. Classrooms are not the only learning environment!

BURNOUT

Anyone can experience job burnout; volunteers too. However, research has shown that working in professions with high job demands and few supports can increase the prevalence of burnout and reduce engagement. Helping professions, such as jobs in health care, teaching, or counselling report high rates of burnout.

Burnout has three main characteristics:

Exhaustion:
The depletion or draining of mental resources.

Cynicism:
Indifference or a distant attitude towards one's job.

Lack of professional efficacy:
The tendency to evaluate one's work performance negatively, resulting in feelings of insufficiency and poor job-related self-esteem.

Source: Canadian Mental Health Association

PB&J MOMENT
(Privilege, Bias & Judgement)

Check Your Lens

People often assume that others think just like them. Open communication will help provide context to explain observed behaviours by both learner and volunteer. It will also make clear what the learner's goals are and what the volunteer's expectations are.

Practice recognizing personal bias by asking: Am I feeling this way/making this decision/suggesting this idea because it is what is best for the learner or because I have decided that it is best for the learner?

Many learners report the most success when they feel respected as adult learners. It is important to avoid paternalizing learners and to remember that they have valuable contributions to make in and beyond the learning process.

PRIORITY & PREFERENCE

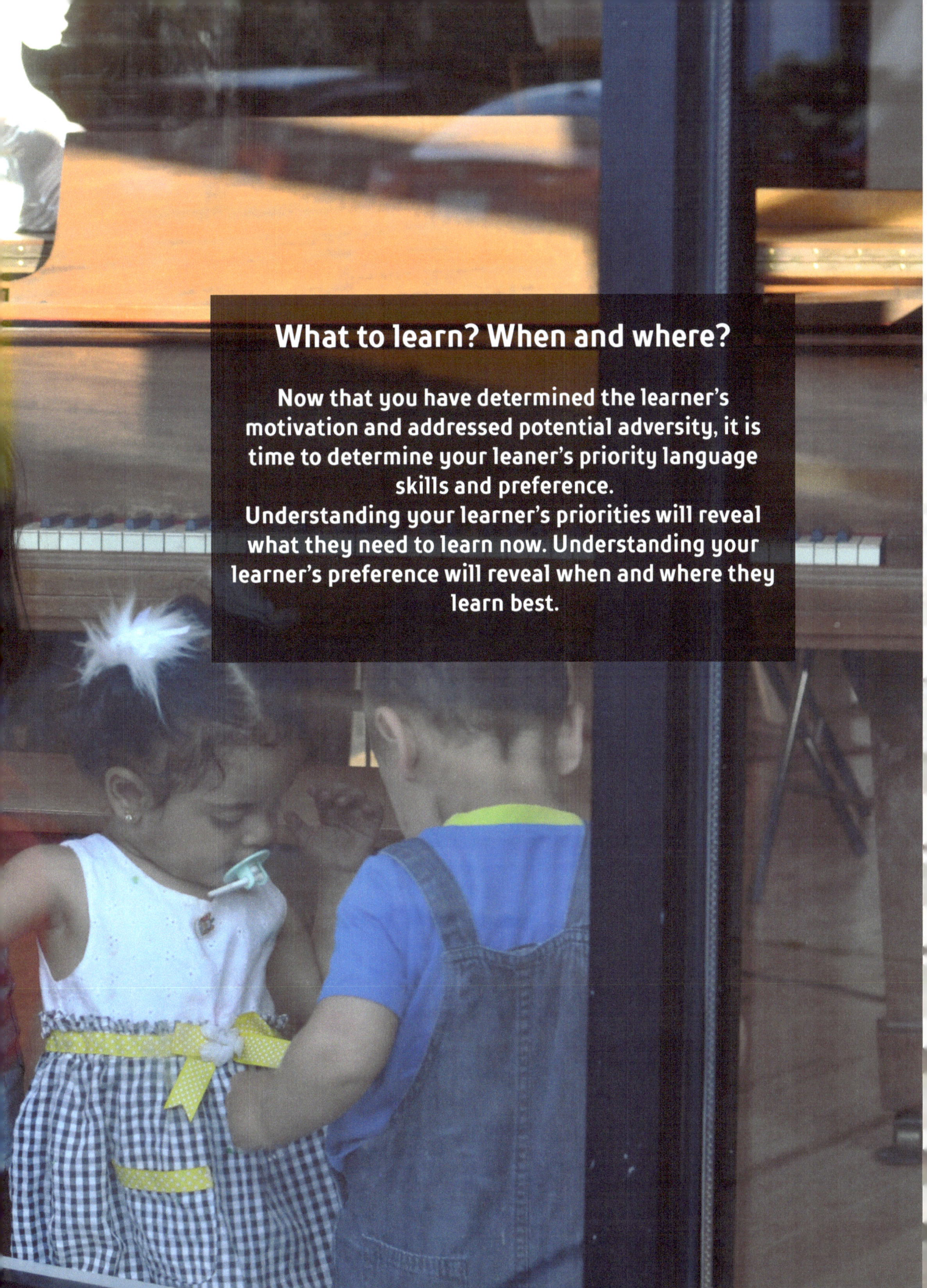

What to learn? When and where?

Now that you have determined the learner's motivation and addressed potential adversity, it is time to determine your leaner's priority language skills and preference.
Understanding your learner's priorities will reveal what they need to learn now. Understanding your learner's preference will reveal when and where they learn best.

PRIORITY LANGUAGE SKILLS

The language learning journey is not a linear process as learners progress through the eight language components. It requires visual, auditory and cognitive skills to build the capacity to communicate information in English either in a productive (writing, speaking) or receptive (reading, listening) manner.

Reading
To understand written symbols

Writing
To use symbols

Speaking
To use spoken language

Listening
To comprehend spoken language

Vocabulary
Words we must know

Grammar
Structure of the language

Pronunciation
Specific sounds

PRIORITY

PREFERENCE: WHAT IS PREFERENCE ABOUT?

People learn in different ways and often have an individual learning preference on how they acquire new knowledge and skills. Adult learners may tend to show a preference according to prior learning experience but may be open to other approaches.

Some learners may prefer watching their teacher show how it is done before joining in; others may prefer joining in right away. Think of the different ways people will approach a dance class: join in from the start or watch how it is done first? Or the ways in which people start using a new program on their cell phone: dive in and figure it out, or go through the instructions first?

What suits one learner very well might now suit another learner. Paying attention to preference will help make the language learning journey viable and sustainable, if not much more enjoyable.

People

Setting/place/space

Time of day

Outdoors/indoors

Taking breaks

Screens/video

Sounds/silence

Sitting/moving

PREFERENCE

MEETING GOALS

It is important to determine the priority of specific language skills the learner requires to achieve their personal goals and purpose. It is equally important to consider the learner's personal preference when forming your learning plan.

Determining which specific language skills are needed provides focus to the language learning journey. It also provides a clear path in choosing materials and resources that are suited to learning those specific language skills. Someone who would like to go to college needs to learn to write in English; someone who would like to join a local yoga class might want to focus on listening skills and specific vocabulary for yoga.

Looking into the learner's personal preference--such as best time of day, places they feel comfortable and people they want to learn with--is also important. If lessons are planned at a time of day when the learner could be distracted, or in a noisy place where they need quiet to learn, it is difficult to succeed. When lessons are delivered in the places and at the times that make sense to the learner, it will build confidence and promote motivation.

When you and the learner can prioritize what they need to learn to meet their goal and do it when and where they prefer, success becomes more likely. For each language priority chosen, you develop a strategy for success that also deeply considers the learner's personal preferences.

This is a traditional collage, scissors and glue, using newspaper pictures (one a news item; the other an ad), a calendar, an image of a marathon race and some construction paper with white bleakness left behind and the cruelty of the barrier constructed at the U.S./Mexico border, complete with razor wire. When I created this, it was November, 2018, and the march had not yet ended. When it did end, these marchers were barred from the U.S. or, if they did enter, they lost their children and were forced to leave the country without them.
"The Wall", Beth Goddard, 2018.

STORYTIME!

An international student is able to read and write quite well academically, but she is not able to chat with local patients she meets during her field placement as part of her Nursing Program. Local colloquialisms aren't in Google Translate!

Together with her volunteer teacher, the student determined her priority to be speaking and listening skills and her preference to practice with native English speakers in the community. A few of the student's classmates have invited her to a local pub for a stand-up comedy night that takes place weekly. After gaining some confidence, she has even joined a local trivia team with locals. Having fun has made her language learning journey even richer.

PB&J MOMENT
(Privilege, Bias & Judgement)

Hold Back Judgement

It is vital for you to accept the many variations of personal priority and preference the learner may present to you. Reserving judgement on how a learner chooses to live their life is paramount to preserving dignity and freedom.

It does not mean that you need to subject yourself to discomfort in order to reach the learner, but it does mean that you need to respect what the learner feels would best suit their personal learning journey. For example, if you are an early riser and the learner's normal routine is getting up later in the morning, the best approach for both of you may be to adopt mid-day or early evening meetings to learn English. Hold back any judgements like "early bird gets the worm" or "wasting the day" that might make your learner feel that their preferences are not important to you, which can derail the connection you have formed and render to less effective.

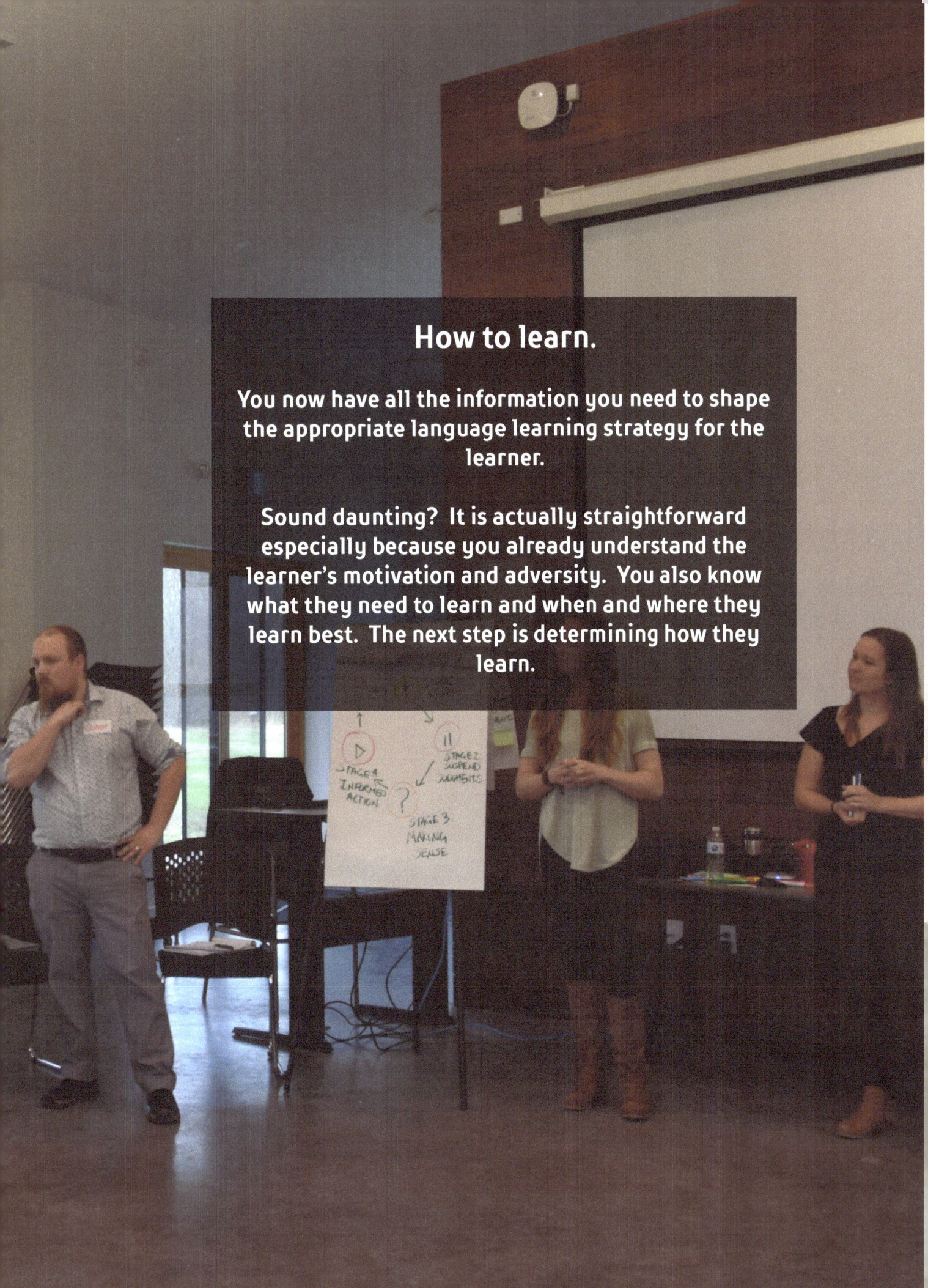

How to learn.

You now have all the information you need to shape the appropriate language learning strategy for the learner.

Sound daunting? It is actually straightforward especially because you already understand the learner's motivation and adversity. You also know what they need to learn and when and where they learn best. The next step is determining how they learn.

CREATING A LEARNING STRATEGY

A learning strategy is made up of exactly what to learn, and how to learn it based on the overarching goals and purpose of why to learn. You need a roadmap to select a set of tactics to build a personalized strategy. Great learning strategies involve four key steps.

- Assess Motivation, adversity, priorities and preferences.
  "Important things about the learner"

- Determine where to begin based on the assessment.
  "Know where to begin"

- Select tactics or learning interventions based on where to begin.
  "Plan to move forward"

- Plan for tracking progress and how to stay focussed.
  "Check in on progress"

ASSESS MAP

MOTIVATION

GOAL	PURPOSE

ADVERSITY

PRIORITY

PRIORITIZED LANGUAGE SKILL	PRIORITIZED PREFERENCE
READING WRITING LISTENING SPEAKING GRAMMAR VOCABULARY PRONUNCIATION EXPRESSIONS	

STRATEGY

This page is designed to be filled in or photocopied and filled in.

ASSESS

The ASSESS graphic helps you MAP the learner's motivation including goal and purpose, identify adversity, and determine priority and preference. There is also a section to add the strategy you form based on MAP.

WHERE TO BEGIN

The WHERE TO BEGIN graphic helps you determine your learner's position on the language learning continuum as it relates to their language learning priority. Find your "you are here" on the graphic.

MOVING FORWARD

The WHERE TO BEGIN graphic also gives you a clear indication of the resources, tactics, and material you need to help the learner move forward on the language learning continuum.

CHECK PROGRESS

Accountability to the learner's goals is essential in order to stay on track and move in a purposeful direction.
Encourage learners to set goals with you that are specific, measurable, attainable, realistic, and time-oriented. When considering whether the commitment required to reach the goal is realistic or not, determine first what is being done now. For example, if someone wanted to set a goal of drinking two litres of water each day, they could set a goal to do that five out of seven days next week. However, if the person is only drinking one glass of water each day now, how likely is it that they would succeed given the distance between now and the new ideal? Perhaps starting with drinking two glasses twice in one week is actually possible. Then, once that is achieved, you can try for four days out of seven until you are drinking two glasses per day seven days per week without fail. No matter what the overarching purpose is that motivates the language learning if the pathway is unrealistic the language journey may not succeed and may discourage the learner and you in a supportive role.

To avoid the learner feeling overwhelmed and abandoning the work, as a result, help them create a system for staying on track and checking in. One helpful method to introduce is to plan to succeed and also plan to fail. Write down a mini goal like in the water example above. Then, write down two consequences you will enact that also feed the learner's overarching purpose. For example, if the learner rewards themselves for meeting the mini goal of journaling in English twice a week with going to an English movie, or going out to eat and ordering in English, they have not only marked the achievement but have done so with a consequence that also feeds the goal to learn English. The second consequence should be an action the learner takes if they did not reach the mini-goal. For example, the learner may be required to write a letter to themselves, or you as the teacher, in English, explaining why they did not have a chance to journal that week. This consequence requires the learner to work on their English skills to compensate for the improvement lost from not following through as planned. Connecting consequences to the goal is another dynamic way to continue learning throughout the journey that is highly personalized to the learner and therefore much more effective.

WHERE TO BEGIN

| ADVANCED | SPECIALIZED | APPLIED | PRACTICAL |

MANY THINGS TO LEARN

FEWER THINGS TO LEARN

WRITING · READING · SPEAKING · LISTENING (PRACTICAL)

WRITING · READING · SPEAKING · LISTENING (APPLIED)

WRITING · READING · SPEAKING · LISTENING (SPECIALIZED)

WRITING · READING · SPEAKING · LISTENING (ADVANCED)

FEWER WAYS TO LEARN

MANY WAYS TO LEARN

WHERE TO BEGIN

Practical

When a newcomer first arrives, everything is different, including the weather, their home, greetings, money, shopping, food, language, culture, etc. It is important to build language learning around the basic information needed to navigate their new local community. For example, if the topic is grocery shopping, go on a field trip with the learner to the local grocery store and introduce English vocabulary for the main items they usually buy. Slowly introduce challenges with other items and other stores or service providers. A typical goal for adults is to gain independence in navigating the local community.

Applied

As the newcomer starts to get familiar with their local surroundings, it follows to apply language learning towards their goals, such as employment, joining a club, or making deeper connections with friends. If the newcomer's goal of employment and experience is centred around painting exterior and interior walls, then great! Add vocabulary around that topic. A typical goal for adult learners may be employment or volunteering in a specific job or with a particular agency.

Specialized

This is where the learning objective is not defined by the learners' needs and interests, but by an outside standardization such as a particular Canadian Language Benchmark towards Canadian Citizenship, passing an entrance exam or performing any regulated work with mandatory processes. A typical goal for adult learners may be passing a written driver's test.

Advanced

When the learning objective is highly specific and formalized, such as higher education and training (university, college, apprenticeship, and co-op placements), the language learning approach becomes universal across the province or country but the ways to learn may narrow into specific methodologies. A typical goal for adults may be to attend college. In this environment, the expectations are universal across Ontario Colleges, but the ways to learn are narrow when we consider lectures, assignments and tests being the traditional methods.

"Spirited Home",
Christine Hall,
Shukraan Community Arts Workshop, Studio Dreamshare, 2019.

STORYTIME!

An ESL teacher has 15 learners in the classroom at varying levels of English. She uses M. A. P. S. as a homework system to provide relevant, individualized, and differentiated ongoing homework assignments.
It takes only 10 to 20 minutes each class for learners to share how their individual language learning journey is going. This also holds the learner accountable for their own learning but respects their preferences.

One learner actually manages 18-20 hours of independent language learning outside class each week. How does he manage this?: With a structured action plan that is specific to his goals and purpose, accommodates his adversities and includes strategies he is able to do by himself.

He says that seeing the results also motivates him to do more because he knows it's working!

PB&J MOMENT
(Privilege, Bias & Judgement)

Respecting the Learner's Pace

One of the most pronounced privileges to consider while helping a learner is the ease and speed of learning.

If you have had positive experiences with learning because your learning style matched the teaching methods you were exposed to, you may default to measuring your impact as a volunteer instructor based on this ease and speed. Try to remember that the learner will set the pace and that slower-than-expected results may not be a reflection of your lack of effort, but simply an expression of the comfortable pace a learner will set for themselves at that moment.

LEARNING TACTIC CARDS

Use this template card to guide you on how to use the following learning tactic cards. You can print and cut these out for your use on the language learning journey with the learner.

TACTIC FOR INTERVENTION

What to try with your learner that considers language skill priority and preference

BEST SUITED FOR

Suggestion on who might be best served by the tactic as described. Keep in mind that these are only suggestions! You may find ways to use the tactic with different learners or use it as inspiration to make up your own!

TACTIC FOR INTERVENTION	BEST SUITED FOR
Anytime the learner is passing the time (at a doctor's office, in line at the bank, etc.) look around and notice 3-5 items not known in English.	Learners who feel that time is a barrier.
Tongue twisters on challenging sounds. Keep practicing. Make this part of a regular routine.	Learners having difficulties with particular sounds.
Ask the learner to count as high and as fast as they can every time they go to the bathroom, the kitchen, walk down the hall, etc.	A competitive learner becoming familiar with their numbers.
Encourage the learner to try and speak only English for 30 minutes every time their family has a meal.	A family with a desire to learn English as a unit.
Try watching favourite TV shows or movies in English.	An avid TV watcher to fit learning into their schedule.

TACTIC FOR INTERVENTION	BEST SUITED FOR
Read a news article in English every day.	An avid learner who wishes to stay updated on local and worldly news.
Journal about daily routines.	Beginner English learners seeking everyday vocabulary.
Listen to English podcasts to and from work, school, while running errands, etc.	Learners who commute on a regular basis.
Listen to an audiobook while sitting on the porch.	Learners who may not have access to transportation.
Listen to English music and read the words to the song while in a parking lot, at home, at work, or at school until the learner can sing along with the song.	Audio learners with busy schedules.

TACTIC FOR INTERVENTION	BEST SUITED FOR
Exercise in English while at the gym or while watching an English at home exercise video.	Active learners wanting to build English into their regular schedule.
Sign up for a dating website or app to meet people.	A single learner looking to expand their social network.
Set your phone, computer, social media accounts, etc. to English.	Learners who regularly use their electronic devices.
When you shower or brush your teeth, read labels on products. For example, "lather, rinse, repeat" on your shampoo bottle. Look up vocabulary you are unsure of; read it again each time you shower.	Learners wanting to build their daily vocabulary quickly.
Watch TV and advertisements in English.	Learners who enjoy matching movies and television series'.

TACTIC FOR INTERVENTION	BEST SUITED FOR
Start a video challenge online or just for yourself to track progress and force yourself to speak English.	Technologically savvy learners thrive on public feedback and encouragement to hold them accountable.
Organize a recipe-sharing potluck event with others. Prepare lists of ingredients and directions for your recipe to share with others. Make a dish to share at an event.	Learners that enjoy cooking as well as eating with others.
Organize a game or card event.	Learners that enjoy social events and know how to play (or willing to learn) card/board games.
Start a club.	A learner that is interested in sharing their hobby with others.
Arrange a movie night with others. Popcorn is a must!	Learners who enjoy films and hosting.

TACTIC FOR INTERVENTION	BEST SUITED FOR
Host and organize an event such as a book exchange or a clothing swap. Charge a non-perishable item to attend. Donate items leftover from the event.	Learners wanting to be involved with charitable organizations or a learner looking for a new wardrobe.
Create an exercise or dance routine to share. Invite others to do the same. Take turns presenting and participating.	Learners who workout regularly and enjoy having physical fitness as part of their lives.
Collaborate with community allies to create a human library for people to share their talents, such as how to tie a tie, cooking skills, artistic talents, or local greetings.	Learners looking to give back to their communities by sharing their talents and organizing others to do the same.
Learn a new skill in English such as skating, skiing, knitting, and painting.	Adventurous learners looking to get more involved with the local community.
Organize discussion groups through social media about subjects the learner is passionate about.	Learners interested in a particular topic that want to continue exploring their interest in English.

TACTIC FOR INTERVENTION Read a book that's difficult to understand. Take 1-3 words or phrases from each page, concentrate on them, and repeat them.	**BEST SUITED FOR** Learners who thrive on a challenge, follow through on goals and are not discouraged easily.
TACTIC FOR INTERVENTION Organize an event, such as a birthday party or potluck, which includes writing, greeting people, facilitation, and accessing local resources.	**BEST SUITED FOR** Organized learners who value celebrations and get-togethers.
TACTIC FOR INTERVENTION Watch videos such as documentaries or TEDx videos about a familiar topic.	**BEST SUITED FOR** A learner who enjoys non-fiction video series and learning new ideas.
TACTIC FOR INTERVENTION Pretend and act out going through the process of buying a car, booking an appointment, or getting a job. Write a cover letter, resume, look at job ads, and visit the local Employment Services Office.	**BEST SUITED FOR** The learner soon going through these situations in real-life to build confidence.
TACTIC FOR INTERVENTION Organize an ESL chat group in a library, church basement, or community centre.	**BEST SUITED FOR** A learner that is looking for consistency in their schedule as well as language partners to help with accountability.

TACTIC FOR INTERVENTION	BEST SUITED FOR
Go to the grocery store.	Learners who want to gain independence within their new community.
Walk from home to children's school and back.	Learners with school-aged children within walking distance of the school.
Visit the bank.	Learners wanting to gain financial independence.
Participate in programs and events hosted by the local library or other community organizations.	Learners seeking opportunities to become more involved in the community.
Visit the Early Years Centre or playgroups.	Learners that are parents of young children.

TACTIC FOR INTERVENTION
Go to local events such as community fairs, music festivals, etc.

BEST SUITED FOR
Learners seeking to meet new people and experience local entertainment.

TACTIC FOR INTERVENTION
Help the learner to find opportunities to volunteer at a local charity or non-profit organization, or a place the learner is interested in working.

BEST SUITED FOR
Learners who want to make meaningful connections with others who share the same passion.

TACTIC FOR INTERVENTION
Visit Tim Horton's or Starbucks.

BEST SUITED FOR
Learners who want to gain confidence in ordering food and beverages in their new community.

TACTIC FOR INTERVENTION
Visit a restaurant where you can sit down to eat.

BEST SUITED FOR
Learners who want to practice regular activities such as ordering at a restaurant while enjoying a meal.

TACTIC FOR INTERVENTION
Visit a bar or pub to interact with others and make friends together.

BEST SUITED FOR
Learners who are outgoing, have a desire to meet new people and practice natural English.

TACTIC FOR INTERVENTION
Host a BBQ in your backyard or attend a BBQ with the learner.

BEST SUITED FOR
Learners who enjoy hosting, building strong relationships, and practicing their greetings and small talk.

TACTIC FOR INTERVENTION
Go for a walk together in the local park, at the beach, or playground; enjoy a walk in nature.

BEST SUITED FOR
Learners who want to find a place in nature to relax and enjoy the beautiful local scenery.

TACTIC FOR INTERVENTION
Watch a hockey or soccer ball game together.

BEST SUITED FOR
Learners who are avid sports fans.

TACTIC FOR INTERVENTION
Go for a drive together to various places and enjoy the scenery.

BEST SUITED FOR
Learners who love to travel and explore new locations, as well as learners striving to get their next driver's license.

TACTIC FOR INTERVENTION
Go for tea, coffee, pizza, or enjoy a potluck meal together and with others.

BEST SUITED FOR
Learners who want to spend time with friends and create lasting relationships with the people they meet, as well as wants to practise their English greetings and everyday conversations.

TACTIC FOR INTERVENTION
Visit the doctor and dentist's office with the learner.

BEST SUITED FOR
Learners who are looking to gain independence in registering and filling out forms, as well as getting to know the local health care norms.

TACTIC FOR INTERVENTION
Participating in a community scavenger hunt.

BEST SUITED FOR
Learners that want to connect with people and begin to navigate their new community.

TACTIC FOR INTERVENTION
Attend a local festival with a friend.

BEST SUITED FOR
Learners who want to spend time with friends and experience local culture.

www.ingramcontent.com/pod-product-compliance
Lightning Source LLC
Chambersburg PA
CBHW040122120526
44589CB00029B/17